EUGENE MIRONICHEV

AI SEARCH ENGINE OPTIMIZATION GUIDE

THE ESSENTIAL GUIDE
TO OPTIMIZING YOUR
WEBSITE FOR MAXIMUM
VISIBILITY IN
AI SEARCH RESULTS

Copyright

AI Search Engine Optimization Guide: The Essential Guide to Optimizing Your Website for Maximum Visibility in AI Search Results by Eugene Mironichev

Legal Disclaimer

Although the author and publisher have made every effort to ensure that the information in this book was correct at press time, the author and publisher do not assume and hereby disclaim any liability to any party for any loss, damage, or disruption caused by errors or omissions, whether such errors or omissions result from negligence, accident, or any other cause. Use this information at your own risk. The author reserves the right to make any changes he deems necessary to future versions of the publication to ensure its accuracy.

Table of Contents

Introduction: The Dawn of a New Search Era

In 2023, Gartner predicted[1] that by 2028, brands' organic search traffic will decrease by 50% or more due to generative AI-powered search. But everything is happening faster, and some popular websites already see up to 75% reduction in clicks!

"Googling Is for Old People" noted the Wall Street Journal[2] in 2024, claiming that the younger generation relies more on ChatGPT than on Google. A year later, as of September 2025, ChatGPT website doubled its popularity receiving almost six billion monthly visitors (equal to the monthly visits of Bing and Amazon combined![3]) and continues to grow. While Google is still getting more than ten times more visitors and it has also joined the AI revolution and provides AI-generated summaries for searches in more than 200 countries and territories[4].

The rise of Artificial Intelligence (AI) is a fundamental transformation of how information is sought, processed, and delivered, and AI integrated with web search represents a natural evolution.

In this guide, I share insights from extensive, continuous analysis and monitoring of how various AI tools behave, exploring the future of SEO and GEO (Generative Engine Optimization). We will dive into what AI-driven

---

[1] https://www.gartner.com/en/newsroom/press-releases/2023-12-14-gartner-predicts-fifty-percent-of-consumers-will-significantly-limit-their-interactions-with-social-media-by-2025

[2] https://www.wsj.com/tech/googling-is-for-old-people-thats-a-problem-for-google-5188a6ed

[3] https://www.similarweb.com/website/chatgpt.com

[4] https://support.google.com/websearch/answer/16011537

search truly means, how it works, its current impact, and most importantly, how you can adapt your strategies to thrive.

Please note that this book focuses more on AI-native platforms (ChatGPT, Claude, Perplexity) than on AI-enhanced traditional search (Google, Bing).

This guide is specifically tailored for digital marketers, content strategists and SEO specialists who need actionable strategies to adapt swiftly to the rapidly expanding territory of AI search. This book also distinguishes itself by focusing not just on the *"what"* but also on the *"why"* and *"how"*, connecting the underlying AI mechanics directly to actionable SEO strategies and practical implementation checklists.

Chapter 1: Beyond Keywords - Understanding the AI Search Revolution

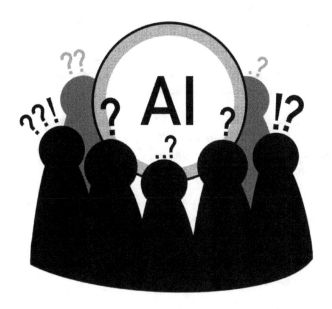

This chapter explores how traditional keyword-based search transforms into an AI-first approach that deciphers user intent and synthesizes comprehensive responses instead of just providing the list of search results.

What exactly *is* AI Search? It's more than just a chatbot plugged into a search engine. Let's look at how the leading players are defining this new paradigm:

- **Google's AI Overview** is focused on providing a snapshot of key information

"AI Overviews provide a snapshot of key information about a topic or question with links so you can easily explore more on the web."[5]

- **Google's AI Mode** - this mode is the kind of **advanced version of "AI Overview"** and emphasizes intelligent organization of information and answering in a simple way. As Google states:

*"AI Mode **intelligently organizes information and answers your question in a simple and intuitive way**, with links to explore more on the web."*[6]

- **ChatGPT Search:** OpenAI focuses on **speed, timeliness** and positions itself in contrast to "traditional" search engines:

*"**Get fast, timely answers** with links to relevant web sources, which you would have **previously needed to go to a search engine for**. This blends the benefits of a natural language interface with the value of up-to-date sports scores, news, stock quotes, and more."* [7]

- **Perplexity AI:** Perplexity centers its definition on the conversational and verifiable nature of the answers:

*"Ask any question, and it searches the web to deliver accessible, **conversational answers backed by verifiable sources**. Each response includes citations and links to original sources [..]"* [8]

- **Anthropic Claude** built-in web-search points to its capabilities of fetching up-to-date information[9]:

---

[5] https://search.google/ways-to-search/ai-overviews/

[6] https://search.google/ways-to-search/ai-mode/

[7] https://help.openai.com/en/articles/9237897-chatgpt-search

[8] https://www.perplexity.ai/help-center/en/articles/10352155-what-is-perplexity

[9] https://docs.claude.com/en/docs/agents-and-tools/tool-use/web-search-tool

*"Answer questions with **up-to-date information beyond its knowledge cutoff**. Claude automatically **cites sources** from search results as part of its answer."*

- **Grok** highlights its access to real-time posts on X (former Twitter):

"Access to real-time public X posts allows Grok to respond to user queries with up-to-date information and insights on a wide range of topics." [10]

While each platform has its nuances, a common thread emerges. The key insight, as derived from these definitions and observing the technology in action, is that AI search isn't just about finding information because more and **more users require and expect more than just a set of blue links**. AI powered interaction involves a sophisticated process that aims to deeply understand the *underlying intent* behind your query, searching across multiple sources, synthesizing that information, and providing a consistent and comprehensive answer with references and citations. It aims to give you not just links but understanding.

Feature	Traditional Keyword-Based Search	AI-Powered Search
Query Processing	Matches exact keywords to indexed documents	Understands the context and user intent even when exact keywords are missing
Search Results Relevance	May return irrelevant search results when keywords are ambiguous or have multiple meanings.	Provides more accurate results from interpreting intent and considering context
Personalization	Personalizes results using location, search history and websites previously visited.	Analyzes broader user interactions (both search and non-search) to deeply understand user preferences and intent
Handling Niche Queries	Niche queries often yield poor results	Breaks down niche queries into simpler sub-queries to provide detailed and relevant response

---

[10] https://help.x.com/en/using-x/about-grok

Feature	Traditional Keyword-Based Search	AI-Powered Search
Refining Search Results	Suggests generic follow up questions without deep personalization	Suggests personalized follow-up questions based on user's previous interactions and current search context

Figure 1.1. Comparison of traditional Keyword-Based Search and AI-powered Intent Recognition Search

With this understanding of how AI search differs from traditional keywords-based search, let's examine how big it is compared to traditional web search leaders.

Chapter 2: How Big is AI Search Compared to Google? Understanding the Landscape

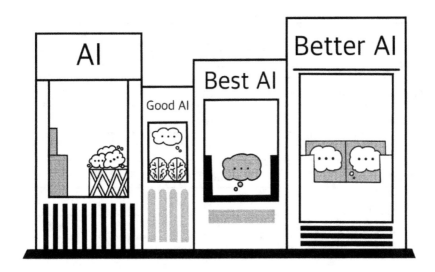

In this chapter we compare metrics of "traditional" search engines and AI-first engines like ChatGPT. This will help to see the increasing significance of AI search and what that means for overall visibility of websites.

Comparing Popularity of AI search engines to Google

Let's see how most popular "traditional" and "AI native" search engines compares by monthly visitors:

Search Engine	Est. Monthly Visitors	In % of total
Google	82.6 billion	85.20%

Search Engine	Est. Monthly Visitors	In % of total
OpenAI ChatGPT	5.9 billion	6.09%
Microsoft Bing	3.5 billion	3.61%
Yahoo	3.0 billion	3.09%
DuckDuckGo	691.9 million	0.71%
Brave Search	375.0 million	0.39%
Deepseek*	333.0 million	0.34%
Grok (X.ai)	191.9 million	0.20%
Perplexity AI	169.5 million	0.17%
Anthropic Claude	157.0 million	0.16%
Poe	15.1 million	0.02%
Meta AI	11.0 million	0.01%

*Figure 2.1. Estimated monthly visits of leading AI sites and search engines (SimilarWeb: snapshot: Sep 2025)[11]. * Deepseek visitors from US are estimated at only 6.52% (21.7 million), according to Similarweb[12]*

Let's break down the numbers:

- AI-powered search is a significant force now, without a doubt anymore.
- Out of the few *"native"* AI engines, OpenAI's ChatGPT is clearly the most popular one. According to research by SimilarWeb, ChatGPT accounts for more than 75% of the combined traffic to the top popular AI tools.[13]
- Google's AI-generated summaries (in *"AI Overviews"*) and fully powered conversations (in *"AI Mode"*) are touching a significant

---

[11] https://www.similarweb.com/

[12] https://www.similarweb.com/website/deepseek.com

[13] https://x.com/Similarweb/status/1920026287625658628

number of visitors because now they are showing on top of the "traditional" keyword based search results for more than 200 countries and territories[14], supporting 40+ languages - a dramatic shift from the US-only rollout in 2024. Google also integrated AI-powered summaries into Google Discover (with about 2 billion users).[15]

- **ChatGPT's Surge:** ChatGPT has rapidly become a major player, not just as a chatbot, but as an information discovery tool. It accounts for almost 5% of Google.com's traffic volume, a staggering figure![16] Its growth is impressive and a fast month-over-month increase. Since 2024, ChatGPT doubled its traffic and, as of October 2025, had almost two times more monthly visitors than Yahoo!

Other Players Growing: Niche players like Perplexity AI and DeepSeek are also demonstrating significant growth. New players like Grok are also aggressively capturing their shares of the search market using their existing large userbases.

The Bottom Line: AI is already involved in a significant portion of online interactions with Google and ChatGPT leading the market. AI search isn't just a future trend, it's a rapidly evolving part of the present digital landscape.

---

[14] https://support.google.com/websearch/answer/16011537

[15] https://techcrunch.com/2025/07/15/google-discover-adds-ai-summaries-threatening-publishers-with-further-traffic-declines/

[16] https://www.similarweb.com/website/chatgpt.com

Chapter 3: Under the Hood: The AI Search Workflow

In this chapter we will break down the process behind AI search into a step by step workflow: from initial user's query input to the final response. You will gain insight into how each stage contributes to delivering more accurate and efficient responses.

How does AI search actually work? It started conceptually as a simple idea of using a Large Language Model (LLM) to summarize traditional search results:

[Search Results] + [AI Summarization] = AI search results ?

However, the process has quickly evolved into a more sophisticated and multi-stage workflow with built-in feedback loop. Let's break down the typical journey of an AI search query:

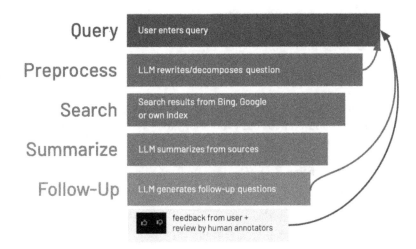

Figure 3.1. General workflow diagram illustrating the stages of an AI search query from input to feedback loop.
(Source: Author graphic based on common AI search processes)

Query Input Step

It begins, as always, with the user entering a search query. This can be anything: a direct question, a keyword phrase, or a specific term.

Pre-processing Step (The AI "Reasoning")

This is where the AI magic starts. Before even searching the web, the LLM often pre-processes the query to optimize performance and accuracy. This can involve:

- **Rewriting** - rephrasing the query for better search engine understanding.

- **Decomposition** - breaking down complex questions into multiple, simpler sub-queries.

- **Formatting** - structuring the query optimally for the underlying search index.

Search Execution Step: The AI then performs an actual web search using one or more indexes. This "index" can be from Google, Bing, Brave Search, an internal web-index (more about it later) or a mix.

Summarization & Synthesis Step: The LLM (AI) analyzes the content retrieved from the selected web sources. It doesn't just copy-paste! it synthesizes the information, combines:

- insights from multiple sources to generate a coherent, comprehensive final answer;
- includes inline citations;
- includes references back to the original websites as inline links or as separate footnotes;

Follow-Up Generation Step (Optional): To facilitate deeper exploration, the AI search engine might generate a set of follow-up questions. These can help the user:

- **Explore the topic** in greater detail.

- **Dive into related areas** of interest.

- **Discover alternative ways** to frame their original query.

- **Feedback Loop:** Continuous improvement is built-in. Users can often provide feedback (e.g., thumbs up/down) on the quality of the answer. Internally, platforms frequently employ human annotators to review and rate responses, further training and refining the AI models.

This systematic process allows AI search engines to move beyond simple keyword matching towards a deeper understanding and more direct fulfillment of user intent.

Query Input Step

The very first step to a search is when a user types a search query using a natural language question in a form of question

- *How puppy food differs from adult*

- *How to ..*

- *Where to ..*

- *What is ..*

- *When ..*

Or in more brief form like *"puppy food vs adult."*

These *"Question-like"* types of search queries appear in up to 52% of all requests according to a few studies.[17][18]

Pre-processing Step: Decoding Intent

AI may instantly consider a request to require a web search based on the input query (like Perplexity AI or Anthropic Claude). Others, like ChatGPT, may require users to explicitly enable *"web search"* mode:

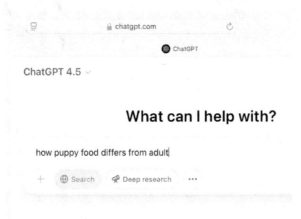

Figure 3.2. ChatGPT interface showing the option to explicitly enable "Search" or "Deep research" modes. (Source: chatgpt.com, accessed Mar 2025)

Let's dive deeper into the fascinating pre-processing step. This initial stage, where the AI rewrites or decomposes the query, reveals much about how these systems interpret user intent.

---

[17] https://moz.com/blog/state-of-searcher-behavior-revealed

[18] https://www.similarweb.com/blog/marketing/seo/top-questions/

Consider this real-world example when a user asks: ***"how adult food differs from puppy food?"***

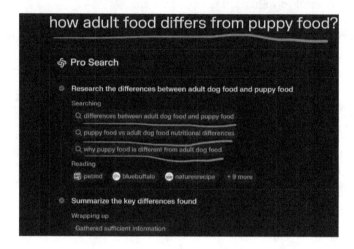

Figure 3.3. Perplexity AI's pre-processing step decomposing the query "how adult food differs from puppy food?" into three specific sub-queries (highlighted). (Source: perplexity.ai, accessed Dec 2024)

Instead of just searching for that exact phrase, the AI's pre-processing step rewrites the query as "*Research the difference between adult dog food and puppy food*" and then intelligently breaks it down into three distinct, more targeted web searches:

1. ***"differences between adult food and puppy food"***: This captures the core, general comparison. It seeks basic differences.

2. ***"puppy food vs adult food nutritional differences"***: Here, the LLM demonstrates understanding. Recognizing the query is about *food*, it specifically probes the *nutritional* aspects, which are key differentiators.

3. ***"why puppy food is different from adult dog food"***: This is particularly insightful. The AI doesn't just want to know *what* the differences are, but *why* they exist. It generates a new question exploring the underlying reasons and rationale behind the formulation differences.

As you can see, the pre-processing isn't just a simple cleanup. It's an active step where the AI refines the query, anticipates related facets (like nutrition), and even generates new angles (the "*why*") to make sure that a comprehensive search is conducted before any answer is synthesized. This multi-query approach allows the AI to gather richer, more relevant information to construct its final response.

Once the web search query (for the original or/and decomposed and rewritten questions) is processed, the AI needs to decide which web pages to "read" to formulate its answer. How does it choose these sources, and how do they compare to traditional search results?

Source Selection: Authority and Overlap

The research[19] comparing the sources cited by Google's AI Overview summaries with the traditional "*blue link*" results for the same query revealed a significant, but not total, overlap: findings suggest this overlap ranges from 33% to 73%. But this overlap can differ significantly depending on the category of the search.

Here is the sample analysis of search results overlap between major AI search engines (for the query "*how puppy food differs from adult*"):

---

[19] https://zapier.com/blog/google-ai-overview-industry-impacts/

↑ Sources

Σ 30 | All Positions ▼ | ⬛ All Engines ▼ → to csv

type to filter by website...

Search...

⬛ All Engines
◇ Google AI Overview [7]
+ Google Gemini [5]
⬛ Perplexity AI [3]
◉ OpenAI ChatGPT [14]
◎ You.com [3]
⚡ Brave Search [3]

✓	Position	Mentions	Website
☐	○ 5 ◉ ⬜	○ 9	petmd.com/dog/nutrition/when-
☐	○ 1.50 ◉ ◎	○ 7	purina.com/articles/dog/puppy/
☐	○ 1 ◇	○ 6	purina.com/articles/dog/puppy/
☐	○ 2 ◎	○ 6	bluebuffalo.com/articles/dog/pu
☐	○ 1 ◉	○ 5	purina.com/articles/dog/puppy/feeding/puppy-food-vs-adult[...]
☐	○ 4 ◎	○ 6	purina.ca/articles/puppy/feeding/when-to-switch-to-adult-[...]
☐	○ 2 ⬛	○ 6	nutrisourcepetfoods.com/blog/pet-parents/when-to-switch-t[...]
☐	○ 3 ◎	○ 4	bettervet.com/resources/pet-nutrition/when-to-switch-a-pu[..]
☐	○ 6 ◎	○ 6	akcpetinsurance.com/blog/is-there-really-a-difference-bet[...]

Figure 3.4. Source analysis tool displaying website mentions and rankings across multiple AI search engines (List View). (Source: aichatwatch.com, accessed Dec 2024)

↑ Sources Graph

Σ 30 | All Positions ▼ | ⬛ All Engines ▼ table

type to filter by website...

Figure 3.5. Source analysis tool displaying the overlap and relationship between sources used by different AI engines (Graph View). (Source: aichatwatch.com, accessed Dec 2024)

Even when AI search engines use the same underlying web index (like Google or Bing), the sources they choose for their answers may differ. *"You need a combination of all, a hybrid."* says[20] *Aravind Srinivas*, founder of Perplexity AI.

Comparing Perplexity AI (Pro)(left) and Google (right) search results:

Figure 3.6. Side-by-side comparison of Perplexity AI (Pro) search sources and Google Search results for the same query. (Source: perplexity.ai, google.com, accessed Dec 2024)

Comparing ChatGPT Search (left) vs Bing (right) search results:

---

[20] https://lexfridman.com/aravind-srinivas-transcript

Figure 3.7. Side-by-side comparison of ChatGPT Search results and Microsoft Bing search results for the same query. (Source: chatgpt.com, bing.com, accessed Dec 2024)

What does this mean? While AI search engines clearly value many of the same *authoritative* sources recognized by other AI and traditional search engines. But at the same time every AI search engine employs its own mix of unique algorithms, ranking signals and criteria to select which sources to use for generating their synthesized answers.

Summarization & Response Synthesis Step

On this step, AI summarizes search results and generates a final answer with links to sources, often prioritizing more authoritative sources. AI summarization mirrors human behavior: if searching for information on *puppy food*, you might trust and check a few well-known veterinary sites and major brand websites first, rather than clicking through dozens of search results! At the same time the summarization also depends on the specific LLM model because every model is trained on different datasets (more about it later). Final response to a user is the summary with inline clickable references to source websites:

I'll answer as the world-famous veterinary nutritionist with the American College of Veterinary Nutrition (ACVN) Diplomate credential.

Puppy and adult dog foods are formulated to meet the distinct nutritional needs of dogs at different life stages. Here's a detailed breakdown: Companion Pet Hospital +9

← →   1/9

Companion Pet Hospital
Transitioning from Puppy Food to Adult Dog Food |
Companion Pet Hospital

Nutritional Differences

1. **Protein & Fat Content**: Puppy foods are higher in protein and fat to support rapid growth and development. For instance, the Association of American Feed Control Officials (AAFCO) recommends that puppy diets contain at least 22.5% protein and 8.5% fat, compared to 18% protein and 5.5% fat in adult dog foods . Companion Pet Hospital   The Spruce Pets +1

2. **Caloric Density**: Puppies require more calories per pound of body weight than adults. Their food is more calorie-dense to meet this demand without overfeeding . K9 of Mine +10

3. **Calcium & Phosphorus**: Essential for bone development, puppy foods have higher levels of calcium and phosphorus. However, excessive amounts, especially in large breeds, can lead to skeletal issues . Arbor Pointe Veterinary Hospital +5   Wikipedia

4. **DHA & Omega-3 Fatty Acids**: Docosahexaenoic acid (DHA) supports brain and eye development in puppies. Many puppy foods are enriched with DHA, often sourced from fish oil . Wikipedia +5   PetMD

Figure 3.8. Response from ChatGPT for "how adult food differs from puppy food"
(Source: chatgpt.com, accessed Apr 2025)

Critically, these clickable inline references are the primary visibility points for driving users from AI search results to your website. Unlike "*traditional*" search results that often display full page titles and descriptions, AI summaries typically only show your *domain name* alongside the cited text (like on this screenshot above) or even hiding inside the group of links inside the dynamic hint that requires users to first hover over the reference, adding an extra click or even two! This additional friction fundamentally reduces click-through opportunities and elevates the importance of building a strong and recognizable brand name.

Follow-up Questions Generation Step

Most AI search engines currently generate few (usually no more than seven questions) follow-up questions that are aimed to engage users into continuing their search and helping them to look deeper into the topic.

Take a look at the set of followup questions generated for *"puppy vs adult food"* search request on Perplexity AI:

In summary, puppy food is specifically designed to meet the nutritional needs of growing puppies, while adult dog food is tailored for maintaining health in fully grown dogs.

⊘ Share   ⟂ Export   ⇄ Rewrite   👍 👎 ⎙ ⋯

⇅ **People also ask**

What are the key nutrients in puppy food that aren't in adult food   +

How does the protein content in puppy food compare to adult dog food   +

Why is more fat included in puppy food   +

How does DHA benefit puppies differently than adults   +

What are the potential health issues if a puppy eats adult dog food   +

Figure 3.12. Follow-up questions generated by Perplexity AI for a puppy food vs adult food query
(Source: perplexity.ai, accessed Apr 2025)

Feedback from User and Review by AI Assessors

Finally, most AI search engines incorporate tools for instant feedback which commonly allows users to indicate satisfaction by clicking on upvote or downvote buttons displayed for each response:

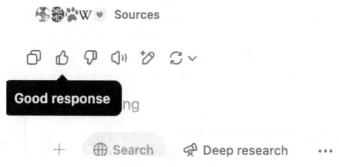

Figure 3.14. Upvoting the response in ChatGPT
(Source: chatgpt.com, accessed Apr 2025)

Unlike *"traditional"* search results this feedback is built into the AI search's iterative improvement process. It allows users to instantly send signals on the quality and helpfulness of received responses. In addition to user votes and using them for so-called reinforcement learning (RL), AI companies also may also employ internal human reviewers[21]. These human reviewers (annotators) may evaluate responses against detailed quality guidelines, checking for accuracy and relevance, safety, and other key criteria to identify areas requiring internal adjustments. Combining feedback from users and internal annotators creates a continuous loop that enables companies to refine their AI and continuously enhance response quality and user satisfaction.

---

[21] https://aws.amazon.com/solutions/case-studies/perplexity-bedrock-case-study/

Chapter 4: The Brains of the Operation: LLMs and Their Knowledge Base

This chapter introduces the internal mechanics of AI search where Large Language Models (LLMs) merges its internal knowledge (based on the training data) with real-time information from web search. It lays the foundation for understanding how AIs generate responses.

At the heart of AI search lies the Large Language Model (LLM), the "smart" assistant that processes information and generates the answers. It summarizes, reviews, and synthesizes data from the selected web sources.

However, the AI's reliance on real-time web search versus its internal knowledge varies.

Example 1: AI answers without a web search enabled

Here is the screenshot where ChatGPT answers for *"how adult food differs from puppy food"* without searching the web by replying solely using its own internal knowledge (in other words, using the dataset it was trained on):

Figure 4.1. Example of a ChatGPT response generated using only its internal knowledge base (web search disabled). (Source: Author's private chat on chatgpt.com, accessed Dec 2024)

Example 2: AI answers with web search enabled

And here is how ChatGPT answer for *"how adult food differs from puppy food"* with *"search"* function explicitly enabled and so it is searching the web and summarizing it in the response as the following:

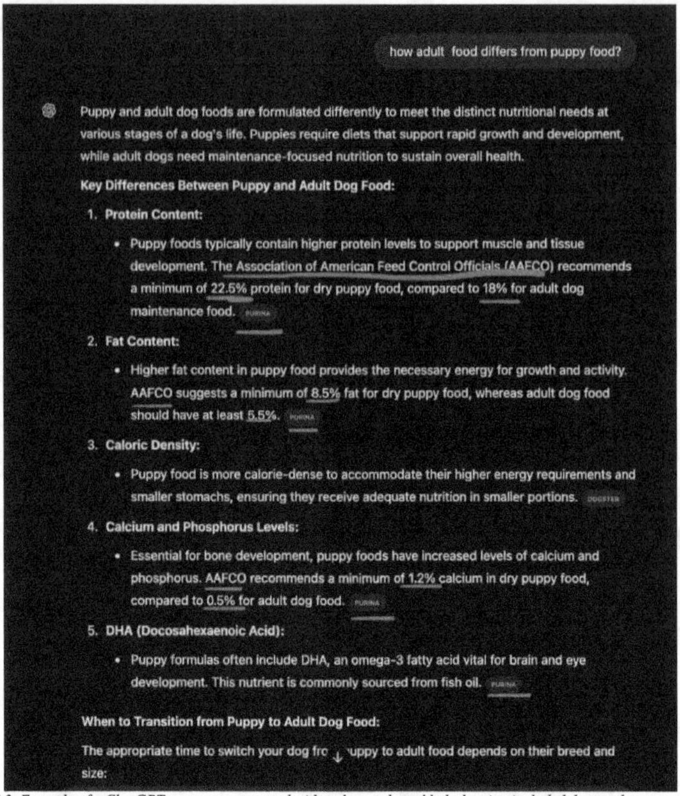

Figure 4.2. Example of a ChatGPT response generated with web search enabled, showing included data and source references (highlighted).
(Source: Author's private chat on chatgpt.com, accessed Dec 2024)

What can we see comparing responses from ChatGPT without and with web search enabled?

- The core information is similar, but the version with web search includes specific numerical data (protein, fat percentages in this case);
- The version with web search also adds references to authoritative sources (like *AAFCO* and *DOGSTER*) extracted from the web search (these references are highlighted on the screenshot).

Also, AI may decide not to run a web search at all for some queries even if it is enabled! Below is the screenshot that shows AI providing an answer to a simple question ("*what is the most stupid joke?*") without referencing to any external web references:

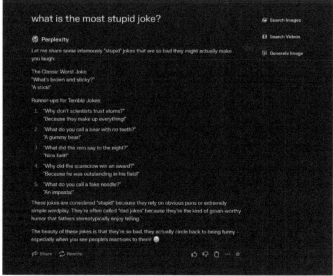

Figure 4.3. Example of a Perplexity AI response without running a web search
(Source: Author's private chat on Perplexity.ai, accessed Dec 2024)

As you see, for some questions, particularly those requiring **factual**, **up-to-the-minute information or specific data points**, the AI makes a decision to run a web search. For requests which are conceptual or creative queries, AI may decide to answer using solely its internal knowledge base.

Supposedly it may skip web search if it understands the query as it is not about some recent events (because AI's internal knowledge is usually about six months out of date) or it is not about rapidly changing topics like stocks, weather and similar subjects.

That is why it is important to have AI models to know about your brand and product not just from a web search but also from its "*brain*", the so called "*Large Language Model*" (LLM) which we will discuss in the next chapter.

Chapter 5: Where Does the LLM's Knowledge Come From?

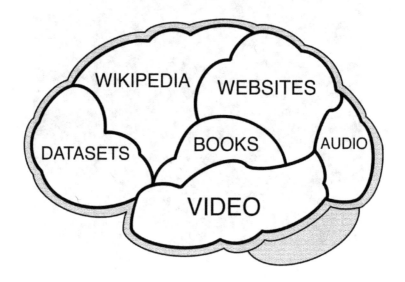

In this chapter we will focus on the origins of LLMs' (Large Language Models) data and will outline the diverse data sources: from massive web crawls to curated sets of books. You will see how each source contributes unique insights and accuracy and directly impacts the reliability of AI-generated content.

Understanding the LLM's training data is key to understanding its capabilities and biases. Let's look at the foundational training data for OpenAI's GPT-3, a model that marked a significant leap in LLM capabilities:

Dataset	Quantity (tokens)	Weight in training mix	Epochs elapsed when training for 300B tokens
Common Crawl (filtered)	410 billion	60%	0.44
WebText2	19 billion	22%	2.9
Books1	12 billion	8%	1.9
Books2	55 billion	8%	0.43
Wikipedia	3 billion	3%	3.4

Figure 5.1. Foundational training dataset composition for OpenAI's GPT-3 model.
(Source: Data adapted from OpenAI research paper - Arxiv:2005.14165[22], accessed Dec 2024)

Common Crawl

This dataset is the largest component of the training data! Think of it as a monthly snapshot of the whole public Internet. It is petabytes in size (one petabyte is 1000 terabytes) and provides a monthly copy of over 2 billion html pages. It is maintained by a non-profit organization called Common Crawl located in California.

Website owners can actually explore this dataset to see what parts of their site are included in this dataset at `index.commoncrawl.org`. You can search your domain, see captured pages, download data segments, and even check the `robots.txt` file Common Crawl saw during its crawl.

Figure 5.2. The Common Crawl Index Server interface, allowing users to search the index by domain pattern.
(Source: index.commoncrawl.org, accessed Dec 2024)

---

[22] https://openai.com/index/language-models-are-few-shot-learners

For example, this search for *.aisearchwatch.com found an compressed zip file with all website pages captured into the dataset for AISearchWatch.com:

```
{"urlkey": "com,aisearchwatch)/demo/ycombinator/2024-10-09-v1-
4dc5370a2e9cbd7b/competitors/index.html", "timestamp":
"20241108054252", "url":
"https://aisearchwatch.com/demo/YCombinator/2024-10-09-v1-
4dc5370a2e9cbd7b/competitors/index.html", "mime": "text/html", "mime-
detected": "text/html", "status": "200", "digest":
"VVQUSGVKIDITSC2FRE3SRLIGLGXEH4EH", "length": "13521", "offset":
"62486754", "filename": "crawl-data/CC-MAIN-2024-
46/segments/1730477028025.14/warc/CC-MAIN-20241108035242-
20241108065242-00333.warc.gz", "languages": "eng", "encoding": "UTF-8"}
{"urlkey": "com,aisearchwatch)/robots.txt", "timestamp":
"20241108054252", "url": "https://aisearchwatch.com/robots.txt",
"mime": "text/plain", "mime-detected": "text/x-robots", "status":
"200", "digest": "4JQWSM7HQLLJ4BS63XEDMRT25AAXXNA7", "length": "878",
"offset": "497868", "filename": "crawl-data/CC-MAIN-2024-
46/segments/1730477028025.14/robotstxt/CC-MAIN-20241108035242-
20241108065242-00044.warc.gz"}
```

Figure 5.3. Example view of data structure within a Common Crawl WARC file, showing captured URL metadata. (Source: index.commoncrawl.org, data view from specific WARC file, accessed Dec 2024)

WebText2 (curated by Reddit)

This dataset contains dozens of gigabytes of content grabbed from links shared and upvoted on Reddit over 15 years. Each page required a minimum of three upvotes to be included, so Reddit users effectively served as curators to filter for higher-quality links. Although this approach yields more curated content than a raw Common Crawl, it may also introduce biases toward the Reddit community's interests, which lean heavily toward entertainment. For instance, *r/funny*[23] forum has around 67 million users, while *r/science*[24] has about 34 million users[25].

Books (Books1 & Books2 datasets)

---

[23] https://reddit.com/r/funny

[24] https://reddit.com/r/science

[25] https://www.reddit.com/best/communities/1/

The Books1 dataset was collected from thousands of fiction books by indie authors on the Smashwords[26] self-publishing platform[27]. The content of the *Books2* dataset was not officially disclosed, but it is believed to contain both public-domain books (published before 1927 and thus no longer under copyright) plus modern copyrighted books. OpenAI later stated that it excluded[28] the Books1 and Books2 datasets from model versions after GPT-3.

Wikipedia

Wikipedia is a large, high-quality, multilingual dataset that covers nearly all human knowledge. Despite its thorough curation, it may still reflect certain editorial or volunteer-driven biases, similar to those found in the broader Wikipedia community. Like WebText2, it was given a higher weighting than some other datasets during AI training[29].

As you see, different sources are given different weights (i.e. importance). Some are more reputable, others are less reputable. But it is easy to see that Wikipedia and WebText2 (which used upvotes from Reddit) acted as reputable sources because they are based on human curated content in one way or another. A similar set of datasets will likely be used for new models in addition to other other reputable sources. While GPT-3 heavily used book corpora, OpenAI later stated that books were explicitly excluded from subsequent training rounds, potentially due to copyright concerns. In recent years, AI developers like OpenAI have actively expanded their training sources through strategic partnerships

---

[26] http://www.smashwords.com

[27] https://authorsguild.org/app/uploads/2023/10/Authors-Guild-Comments-AI-and-Copyright-October-30-2023.pdf

[28] https://www.businessinsider.com/openai-destroyed-ai-training-datasets-lawsuit-authors-books-copyright-2024-5

[29] https://gregoreite.com/drilling-down-details-on-the-ai-training-datasets

Dataset	Quantity (tokens)	Weight in training mix	Epochs elapsed when training for 300B tokens
Common Crawl (filtered)	410 billion	60%	0.44
WebText2	19 billion	22%	2.9
Books1	12 billion	8%	1.9
Books2	55 billion	8%	0.43
Wikipedia	3 billion	3%	3.4

Figure 5.4. Logos representing some of OpenAI's strategic partners for acquiring training data, including publishers and online platforms. (Source: Logos property of respective companies; compiled by author to illustrate Open AI's partnerships [30] [31] [32])

- **Major Publishers:** deals with News Corp, Axel Springer, TIME, The Atlantic, The Wall Street Journal, Financial Times, and others provide access to high-quality, curated news and editorial content[33] [34].

- **Online Platforms:** partnerships with Reddit (community discussions), Stack Overflow (technical Q&A, code), and Shutterstock (image descriptions, visual context) add diverse, specialized data.

This hybrid approach for collecting training from both public and closed sources serves two purposes:

---

[30]https://aibusiness.com/nlp/openai-inks-licensing-deal-with-news-corp-for-chatgpt-training-data

[31]https://developers.google.com/search/docs/fundamentals/creating-helpful-content

[32]https://www.searchenginejournal.com/meta-integrates-google-bing-search-results-into-ai-assistant/514291/

[33]https://aibusiness.com/nlp/openai-inks-licensing-deal-with-news-corp-for-chatgpt-training-data

[34]https://www.fastcompany.com/91130785/companies-reddit-news-corp-deals-openai-train-chatgpt-partnerships

- Allows to maintain broad coverage from the public web (through datasets like *Common Crawl*);
- Strategically incorporates high-quality, verified, and often more current information from trusted partners. This directly impacts the knowledge base AI search engines draw upon.

Understanding sources of AI training data offers important insights into the strengths and limitations of modern LLMs which serve as the "brains" behind AI with and without web search. With this background in mind, we will now discuss how to produce content in a way that AI will best understand and remember.

Chapter 6: Optimizing Content for Easy Understanding By AI

In this chapter we will go into some practical strategies for making your content more tailored to AI. We will review essential techniques such as intent-based writing, the usage of long-tail and semantic keywords, and the role of framing content around questions and including FAQ sections into your website.

Given that content from websites feeds both traditional search crawlers *and* AI training datasets/live searches, how can we optimize our content specifically for this new AI-driven search? Let's explore key strategies, drawing on recommendations from experts like Fabrice Canel, Principal Product Manager at Bing[35]:

---

[35]https://www.linkedin.com/posts/fabricecanel_ai-search-is-revolutionizing-the-way-customers-activity-7264404571949531137-HzCQ

Focus on Intent-Based Content:

Go beyond simply matching keywords like *"puppy leash training"* Dig deeper to understand and address the *user's underlying goal or intent.*

Example: Instead of a generic page titled *"Puppy Leash Training"* create content like *"A Step-by-Step Guide to Successfully Leash Train Your Puppy (and Solve Common Problems)"*

This directly addresses the user's likely intent-learning the process effectively and overcoming potential hurdles rather than just defining the term. Focus on the practical *"how-to"* and problem-solving aspects.

Additional Examples:

In SaaS and Tech:

Instead of just targeting *"Cloud Storage Features"*, create content titled *"Choosing the Best Cloud Storage Plan: A Guide for Freelancers and Small Teams"* that addresses the user's goal of selecting the right service.

In Finance:

Rather than a page on *"Retirement Accounts"* focus on user intent with *"How to Open Your First IRA: Roth vs. Traditional Explained"* guiding users step-by-step through the decision and action process.

Leverage Long-Tail Keywords:

Utilize specific, detailed phrases that capture the user's situation and intent more precisely.

Example: Instead of the broad term

"leash training" target more specific phrases like *"positive reinforcement leash training for stubborn puppies"*, *"how to stop a puppy pulling on the leash during walks"* or *"getting an anxious puppy comfortable with the harness"*

These longer phrases often attract users with very specific needs and may face less competition.

Additional Examples:

In E-commerce:

instead of *"running shoes"* target these: *"best lightweight running shoes for marathon training", "waterproof trail running shoes with wide toe box"*

In Travel:

rather than *"hotels in London"* target these: *"family-friendly hotels near London Eye with pool", "boutique hotels in Covent Garden under £200"*

Embrace Conversational Keywords

Try to mirror the natural language patterns people use when searching or asking questions, especially in voice search or AI chats.

Example: incorporate phrases like

"What's the best way to get my puppy used to the leash?" or *"My puppy hates the leash, what do I do?"* within your content, ideally providing direct answers. Aim for a helpful and *natural* tone rather than just listing keywords!

Additional examples:

In SaaS and Tech industries:

include phrases like *"How much does Slack cost per user?"* or *"Can I integrate Mailchimp with Salesforce?"* directly addressing common user queries.

Local Service (for example, Plumber):

write content answering *"What to do if my basement is flooding?"* or *"Signs I need to replace my water heater"*

Utilize Semantic Keywords

Include related terms, concepts, tools, and ideas that help AI understand the broader context of your topic.

Example: when discussing incorporate related terms such as

"puppy leash training", *"positive reinforcement"*, *"dog harness vs collar"*, *"puppy socialization"*, *"loose-leash walking"*, *"high-value treats"* and *"consistency in training"*

This builds topical authority and helps AI grasp the full scope of the subject.

Additional examples:

In e-commerce:

Instead of *"running shoes"* target *"best lightweight running shoes for marathon training"*, *"waterproof trail running shoes with wide toe box"*

In Travel:

rather than *"hotels in London"* target *"family-friendly hotels near London Eye with pool"*, *"boutique hotels in Covent Garden under £200"*

Frame Content Around Questions

Structure key information as answers to the questions people naturally ask about the topic.

Example: use headings for sections like *"When should I start leash training my puppy?"* or *"How long should leash training sessions be?"*

Additional Examples:

In e-commerce (for example, selling cameras):

structure content with headings like: *"What's the difference between DSLR and mirrorless cameras?"*, *"Which lens is best for portrait photography?"* or *"How do I clean my camera sensor?"*

In SaaS and Tech:

organize a help document using questions:

"How do I reset my password?", *"Can I export my data?"* or *"What are the system requirements?"*

Create FAQ or PPA Section

Create dedicated *"Frequently Asked Questions (FAQ)"* or *"People Also Ask (PPA)"* sections to address common concerns directly. Here is the example of such dedicated FAQ page:

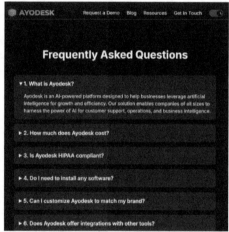

Figure 6.2. Screenshot of Ayodesk.com, showing the dedicated FAQ page. (Source: ayodesk.com, accessed April 2025)

For important pages (like a product or pricing pages) you may also add FAQ sections at the bottom of the pages. Below is the screenshot of the *embedded* FAQ section at the bottom of the blog post:

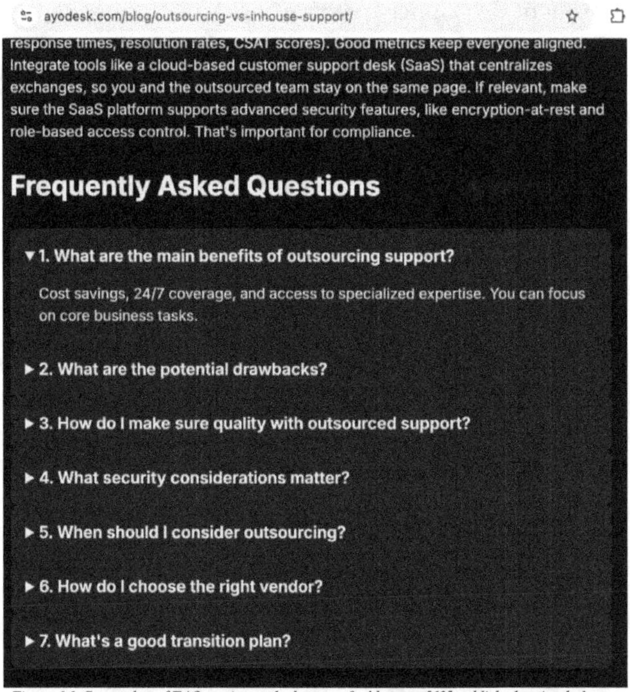
ayodesk.com/blog/outsourcing-vs-inhouse-support/
response times, resolution rates, CSAT scores). Good metrics keep everyone aligned. Integrate tools like a cloud-based customer support desk (SaaS) that centralizes exchanges, so you and the outsourced team stay on the same page. If relevant, make sure the SaaS platform supports advanced security features, like encryption-at-rest and role-based access control. That's important for compliance.
Frequently Asked Questions
▼ 1. What are the main benefits of outsourcing support?
Cost savings, 24/7 coverage, and access to specialized expertise. You can focus on core business tasks.
▶ 2. What are the potential drawbacks?
▶ 3. How do I make sure quality with outsourced support?
▶ 4. What security considerations matter?
▶ 5. When should I consider outsourcing?
▶ 6. How do I choose the right vendor?
▶ 7. What's a good transition plan?
Figure 6.1. Screenshot of FAQ section at the bottom of a blog post[63] published at Ayodesk.com. (Source: ayodesk.com, accessed April 2025)

In addition to "*embedded*" FAQ sections on every page it is still good to publish a general FAQ page.

Tools to quickly create FAQ or PPA

First of all, you may ask AI chats about your product or service and draw inspiration from "*People Also Ask*" (PAA) or "Follow Up" questions in AI chats results like the one you see in AI chats.

You may also generate FAQ sections along with all required HTML code using tools like ChatGPT. I've added an open-source plugin for ChatGPT called "*AI (FAQ) Generator*"[36] that you may use right from ChatGPT. Here

[36] https://chatgpt.com/g/g-67fa6fe6bb3c8191953a5954699a2325-ai-faq-generator-open-source

is the screenshot of FAQ it may produce based on the website link you gave it:

make faq for ayodesk.com

Certainly! Based on the information available on ayodesk.com, here are 12 frequently asked questions (FAQs) that summarize and clarify key aspects of Ayodesk's offerings:

```markdown
markdown                                                    ⎘ Copy    ✐ Edit

### Ayodesk Frequently Asked Questions (FAQs)

1. **What is Ayodesk?**
   Ayodesk is an AI-powered customer support platform designed for small teams and startu

2. **Who is Ayodesk designed for?**
   Ayodesk is tailored for small companies and startups seeking an intuitive, affordable,

3. **What are the key features of Ayodesk?**
   Key features include:
   - Affordable and transparent pricing
   - Simple and intuitive interface
   - Enterprise-grade security
   - High customizability
   - HIPAA compliance options
   - API access and integrations with tools like Zapier and GitHub

4. **How does Ayodesk ensure data security** ↓
```

Figure 6.4. Screenshot of the response from Ayodesk Frequently Asked Questions (FAQ) Generator in ChatGPT, showing generating FAQ questions. (Source: chatgpt.com, accessed April 2025)

Creating FAQ sections is the strategic approach that moves beyond *simple* keyword matching! It prioritizes creating comprehensive, well-structured content that *directly* answers the user's underlying questions.

Checklist 1: Content Optimization for AI Understanding

Purpose: check that content aligns with AI priorities:

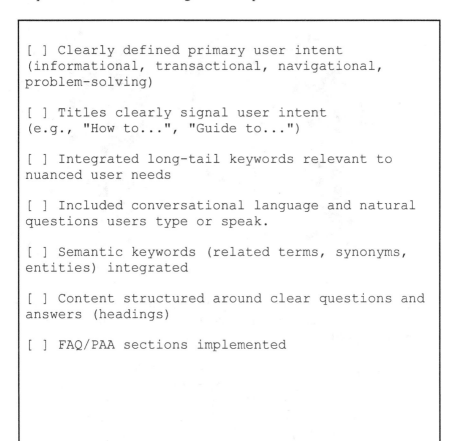

[ ] Clearly defined primary user intent (informational, transactional, navigational, problem-solving)

[ ] Titles clearly signal user intent (e.g., "How to...", "Guide to...")

[ ] Integrated long-tail keywords relevant to nuanced user needs

[ ] Included conversational language and natural questions users type or speak.

[ ] Semantic keywords (related terms, synonyms, entities) integrated

[ ] Content structured around clear questions and answers (headings)

[ ] FAQ/PAA sections implemented

Chapter 7: Technical SEO for the AI Era

In this chapter, you'll learn essential technical strategies for getting your website (and its content) accessible and indexable by AI crawlers. We will review and explore:

- Using `/robots.txt` to guide AI and non-AI crawlers;
- What is *Server-Side Rendering (SSR)* and its advantages over *Client-Side Rendering (CSR)* and why it is very important;
- How to properly implement and use embedded structured data;
- How to re-index your website for AI search engines;

Beyond content strategy, technical optimization is very critical to ensure that AI can effortlessly access, understand, and index your website's information. Let's explore the key technical considerations:

Robots.txt: Rules For Bots (with Cautions)

The `/robots.txt` file is the traditional way to provide instructions to web crawlers about which parts of your site they should or shouldn't access.

How `robots.txt` works:

- This */robots.txt* a simple plain text file uploaded to your web-site into the root folder;
- This file contains the list of blocks where each one starts with the identifier of a web bot (aka *"User-Agent"*) and path or a path mask to tell where this bot is allowed (*"Allow"* command) to go and where it is not allowed (*"Disallow"* command).

  Example of such block:

  ```
  User-agent: CCBot
  Allow: /blog/?
  Disallow: /login/*
  ```

- Bots running by AI and by search engines are supposed to respect these rules but they are not legally obliged to do so, and compliance is completely voluntary! Moreover, there are publications about suspecting some web scraping bots (which are ran by search engines and AI companies) not respecting these rules in some case practice[37].

- Major content management systems like WordPress and similar have predefined *robots.txt* file with predefined set of rules;

Here are some of the most active bots used by AI companies and their data providers:

---

[37]   https://www.businessinsider.com/openai-anthropic-ai-ignore-rule-scraping-web-contect-robotstxt

- **CCBot** - the bot from *Common Crawl* which captures content for the large dataset used by all large AI companies;
- **GPTBot, OAI-SearchBot** - web bots used by OpenAI, the company behind ChatGPT[38]
- **PerplexityBot, PerplexityUser** - web bots used by Perplexity AI for indexing content and running a search on a given website[39]
- **ClaudeBot, Claude-User, Claude-SearchBot** - web bots used[40] by Claude AI by Anthropic

Here is an example from Wall Street Journal's *robots.txt*[41] which attempts to block specific AI crawlers (like *CCBot* which is used by the *Common Crawl* dataset, *anthropic-ai*, *ClaudeBot*, *Google-Extended*) from reading content on wsj.com website. WSJ explicitly don't allow AI bots to read their content:

Figure 7.1. Screenshot of /robots.txt file at The Wall Street Journal's website, showing directives aimed at blocking various AI crawlers. (Source: https://www.wsj.com/robots.txt, accessed Dec 2024)

[38] https://platform.openai.com/docs/bots
[39] https://docs.perplexity.ai/guides/bots
[40] https://support.claude.com/en/articles/8896518-does-anthropic-crawl-data-from-the-web-and-how-can-site-owners-block-the-crawler
[41] https://wsj.com/robots.txt

Don't rely on robots.txt for protecting content

While *robots.txt* remains an important technical standard so do **not** rely on robots.txt as your sole defense! If you need to prevent AI or any other web crawlers from accessing certain content, pages or folders then you must also protect access to your content with other methods (like login walls or IP blocking). Use authentication controls for true protection.

How to quickly create or verify Robots.txt for your website

The fastest and easiest way to verify `robots.txt` and generate (if needed) is to use AI like ChatGPT. I've created a free open-source plugin called "*AI Robots.txt Assistant*"[42] that you may run right from ChatGPT.

For verifying `robots.txt` file, you can use online tools like Google's own Robots.txt Tester[43]. To dig deeper check the "*Introduction to Robots.txt*"[44] guide from Google for the detailed information on how to update and define rules in `robots.txt`.

Server-Side Rendering For Accessibility

Dynamic JavaScript-heavy websites (also called **C**lient-**S**ide **R**endering or CSR), where JavaScript primarily renders content in the user's browser, can significantly slow down indexing and require more resources from crawlers because it requires crawler to run some kind of full modern browser to render a web page. That is why SSR (**S**erver-**S**ide Rendering), where a server is doing a heavy lifting of rendering the page and sends a complete HTML page to a browser without requiring browser itself to compute lot of things, is strongly preferred if you want your pages to be indexed by AI and search engines. If a

---

[42]   https://chatgpt.com/g/g-67f24f57898c8191a5106a78ca9f85eb-ai-robots-txt-assistant-open-source

[43] https://search.google.com/search-console/settings/robots-txt

[44] https://developers.google.com/search/docs/crawling-indexing/robots/intro

website uses SSR then AI's bot can simply "download" the content of the page with a very simple script on a very simple and minimal server with super limited and minimal resources but running a full browser requires a modern computer.

Tests and analysis[45] conducted by Vercel (cloud hosting company) suggested that only web crawlers from very experienced and large companies like Google and Apple are actually capable of rendering dynamic javascript into a final page. But web crawlers from ChatGPT, Anthropic Claude, Common Crawl (super-large dataset for AI training) do not render Javascript inside pages. What does it mean? It means that if your website is programmed with so-called "*modern and dynamic javascript*" then it's highly likely AI bots won't see its content fully.

Also, there is a very significant 7x difference in speed of indexing required for such websites. In one case study[46] shared by *Onely* marketing agency it took Google approximately 2 weeks to re-index complex JavaScript pages, compared to just 2 days (seven times faster!) for static HTML versions of the same content. Note that these results are context-dependent and may not apply to websites with real-time information.

Feature	Server-Side Rendering	Client-Side Rendering
Indexing Speed	1-2 days	~2 weeks
Resources Required For AI to Read	Low (just downloads html)	High (need to fully render)

---

[45] https://vercel.com/blog/the-rise-of-the-ai-crawler

[46] https://www.onely.com/blog/google-needs-9x-more-time-to-crawl-js-than-html/

Feature	Server-Side Rendering	Client-Side Rendering
Support By Web Bots	<ul><li>Google</li><li>Bing</li><li>Common Crawl</li><li>OpenAI ChatGPT</li><li>Anthropic Claude</li><li>all others</li></ul>	<ul><li>Google</li><li>Bing</li><li>Apple</li></ul>

Figure 7.3. Table comparing how server-side rendered and client-side rendered pages are accessible to AI and non-AI bots. (Source: multiple sources)

Because of all of it altogether, implementing SSR (Server-Side Rendering), where the server sends a fully rendered HTML page to the browser/crawler, dramatically improves crawl efficiency and indexing speed.

How to check if your website is accessible by search engines

One very simple approach for quickly checking if your website is SSR or not by looking if your website can change content without reloading a page in a browser is to open the *"source code"* (using *right-click -> Inspect* in your browser): if you see some scrambled programming code then highly likely your website is not using SSR. Another way is to temporarily turn off javascript in a browser and test how a website shows without javascript enabled: can you see the original content and text?

But the best way is to use Google Search Console and its "URL Inspection" tool[47] that can show what a bot from Google (and similar bots from other

---

[47] https://search.google.com/search-console/inspect

search engines and AO) will see for a specific page on your website. Here is the example of using this tool for a website:

Figure 7.4. The Google Search Console - URL Inspection for Ayodesk.com/blog url.
(Source: chatgpt.com/gpts, accessed Apr 2025)

Sitemap.xml: Map To Your Website

`sitemap.xml` is a special structured data file that contains links to all pages on your website that should be indexed. Most modern CMS systems, like Wordpress, are generating and updating this file automatically. AI and traditional search engines are looking into this file as a map to the website.

Check if the sitemap for your website is up-to date and available at `www.yourwebsite.com/`**`sitemap.xml`**

Sitemap.xml for large websites

If your website is large and frequently updated then instead of re-generating sitemap for every update you may setup `sitemap.xml` entries with indicated update frequency like the template below. This way bots will know when to re-index your website again:

```
<urlset xmlns="http://www.sitemaps.org/schemas/sitemap/0.9"
xmlns:xhtml="http://www.w3.org/1999/xhtml">

<url>

<loc>https://yourwebsite.com/</loc>

<changefreq>daily</changefreq>

<priority>1.0</priority>

</url>

<url>

<loc>https://yourwebsite.com/blog</loc>

<changefreq>daily</changefreq>

<priority>1.0</priority>

</url>

</urlset>
```

(Source: adapted from sitemaps.org standard structure[56])

If you don't have `sitemap.xml` then first check why it is not generated by the content management system you most likely use? Modern website engines like Wordpress, Webflow, Ghost and all the others already do support generating `sitemap.xml` automatically.

JSON-LD: The Linchpin of AI Search Visibility

JSON-LD (**J**ava**S**cript **O**bject **N**otation for **L**inked **D**ata), often called *"Semantic JSON"* or *"Structured Data"*, involves embedding machine-readable **structured** snippets with the content inside your page's HTML.

These structures may explicitly describe the content and context of your page (e.g., this is an article, this is a recipe, this is a product with its price). This approach allows crawlers to quickly understand the page's meaning directly without complex parsing or rendering.

Sample JSON-LD for AIChatWatch.com:

```json
{

  "@context": "https://schema.org",

  "@type": "Organization",

  "name": "AI Chat Watch",

  "url": "https://aichatwatch.com",

  "description": "AI Chat Watch is an free open-source tool for tracking
what AI like ChatGPT say about brands, companies, products, industry.",

  "contactPoint": {

    "@type": "ContactPoint",

    "contactType": "customer support",

    "url": "https://aichatwatch.com/contact"

  }

}
```

The importance of structured data, particularly in the form of JSON-LD, warrants a dedicated focus. It is arguably one of the most critical technical elements for success in visibility for AI. Structured data is effectively your website and your content already parsed and ready for copying into a database of a search engine or AI scanner. Without structured data, AI and search engines have to render, parse your website which involves much more computing resources and takes more time.

Why is JSON-LD so Essential?

Quick analysis shows that almost all top-performing sources referenced in AI search results utilize JSON-LD. It also consistently shows that top-performing content appears in AI search results (both in Google's AI Overviews and as primary sources for AI answers) and shares a common trait: robust implementation of JSON-LD structured data.

Look at the example below for the query "*how to drink water*" Google's AI Overview and the traditional "featured snippet" both reference the *same page* from *Healthshots.com*[48]. This page, like most top-ranking content, effectively uses JSON-LD:

Figure 7.6. Google Search results page for "how to drink water" displaying both the AI Overview and traditional featured snippet referencing the same source (Healthshots.com). Annotations indicate Google's AI Overview and Featured Snippet. (Source: google.com, accessed Dec 2024)

The same website uses JSON-LD extensively to represent both the content of the page and content of FAQ section:

---

[48] https://www.healthshots.com

Figure 7.7. Healthshots.com article page alongside browser developer tools showing the underlying HTML source code containing JSON-LD snippets. (Source: healthshots.com, accessed Dec 2024)

Types of JSON-LD Structures:

JSON-LD allows you to embed snippets of code (usually in the <head> section of your HTML but also can be inside the main body too) that explicitly define the type and properties of your content in a machine-readable format. Looking at the source code example from the Healthshots website, we can these JSON-LD snippets:

```
<script type="application/ld+json">
                   {
            "@context": "http://schema.org",
            "@type": "HowTo",
            "mainEntityOfPage": "https://www.healthshots.com/how-to/know-
why-and-how-to-drink-water-the-right-way/",
            "inLanguage": "en",
            "name": "Have you been drinking water the right way? Know how
to do it",
            "description": "Do you drink water with your meals? Well, you
have been doing it wrong. Know how to drink water the right way.",
            "url": "https://www.healthshots.com/how-to/know-why-and-how-
to-drink-water-the-right-way/",
            "totalTime": "",
            "tool": "",
            "image": {
            "@type": "ImageObject",
            "url":
"https://images.healthshots.com/healthshots/en/uploads/2022/10/31171343/WATER-
1600x900.jpg",
            "height": 1600,
            "width": 900                        },
            "step": [{
                    "@type": "HowToStep",
                    "text":"1. Always try to have lukewarm water
    Warm or hot water actually has the ability to absorb deeper into your tissues
Warm water cleanses and detox's your body better than the cold or normal water.
Ice cold water is an absolute disaster for your health as it can give you cold or
cough problems and can also dampen your digestion. Warm foods promote digestion
while cold foods hinder it.
            "
            },{
                    "@type": "HowToStep",
                    "text":"2. Sit down while drinking water
    Standing and drinking disrupts the balance of body fluids. You may accumulate
unwanted excess fluid in your body if you drink while standing up which can often
```

Figure 7.8. *Close-up view of JSON-LD code within the Healthshots.com source, detailing @type, step, and other properties for the "HowTo" schema. (Source: healthshots.com, accessed Dec 2024)*

This JSON-LD structure on the screenshot:

- **Clearly defines the page type:** @type: "HowTo" tells the crawler this page provides instructions.

- **Structures step-by-step instructions:** The step property organizes the "how-to" guide logically.

- **Provides necessary metadata:** Includes the name (title), description, and image information in a structured way.

- **Enable understanding without rendering:** Crucially, crawlers can parse this JSON-LD data and understand the page's core content and structure *without needing to execute complex JavaScript or fully render the page.*

- **Maintains human readability:** While machine-readable, the code remains relatively understandable to developers.

Common JSON-LD Structures

There are 815 types of JSON-LD structures[49], and here are some of the most commonly used ones:

- **WebPage**: For general pages, providing basic metadata.

- **Article**: For news articles, blog posts, including author, publication date.

- **HowTo**: For instructional content, outlining steps.

- **QAPage & FAQPage**: For question-and-answer formats.

- **Event**: For time-based content (concerts, webinars).

- **Review**: For product or service reviews, including ratings.

- **Product**: For e-commerce, detailing product name, price, availability, brand.

Finding existing JSON-LD inside any page

You can easily check if any page uses JSON-LD:

- Open your browser's developer tools (usually F12 or right-click > Inspect).

- View the page source code.

- Search for "`schema.org`" (the vocabulary standard used by JSON-LD). This will reveal any implementations of JSON-LD if any.

---

[49] https://www.schema.org

Creating JSON-LD

- **CMS (Content Management System) Support:** Most major Content Management Systems (like WordPress, Shopify, Webflow) offer built-in JSON-LD support or 3rd party plugins/extensions available to easily add it to every page.

- **AI Assistance:** Tools like ChatGPT, Claude and others can help generate JSON-LD snippets using HTML or text provided to them.

Selecting Proper JSON-LD Types

The official schema.org website[50] (www.schema.org) is the definitive resource for exploring more than 800 structure types and their properties.

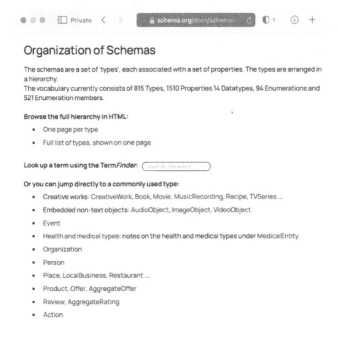

Figure 7.9. Screenshot of schema.org website with the list of JSON-LD types available . (Source: schema.org, accessed Apr 2025)

---

[50] https://www.schema.org

Selecting the most specific relevant schema types (e.g., choosing **HowTo** for a tutorial instead of **Article** or **WebPage**) provides clearer context to AI. Using a more suitable type also improves understanding of the content and the likelihood of your content being used effectively by AI.

Multiple JSON-LD structures

A single page may leverage multiple JSON-LD types working together. Previously discussed *"how to drink water"* page actually uses multiple structures:

- **WebPage** (basic page info)

- **HowTo** (the core instructional content)

- **BreadcrumbList** (showing the page's position in the site hierarchy)

- **SiteNavigationElement** (defining how the page connects to other site sections)

Testing that page with Schema Markup Validator[51] validator.schema.org shows the following detected items:

---

[51] https://validator.schema.org

Detected	0 ERRORS	0 WARNINGS	5 ITEMS
WebPage	0 ERRORS	0 WARNINGS	1 ITEM
HowTo	0 ERRORS	0 WARNINGS	1 ITEM
BreadcrumbList	0 ERRORS	0 WARNINGS	1 ITEM
Article	0 ERRORS	0 WARNINGS	1 ITEM
SiteNavigationElement	0 ERRORS	0 WARNINGS	1 ITEM

Figure 7.10. Results from the Schema Markup Validator tool for the Healthshots.com page, confirming the detection of multiple schema types (WebPage, HowTo, BreadcrumbList, etc.). (Source: validator.schema.org, accessed Dec 2024)

Validating JSON-LD implementation

Always validate your implementation:

- Google Rich Results Test[52]: Checks if your page supports rich results and validates the structured data.

- Schema Markup Validator[53]: A general validator for schema.org markup, checking for errors and warnings. Aim for zero errors and warnings for optimal implementation.

Again, the key advantage of JSON-LD is efficiency! Search engine crawlers can parse this structured information far more easily than interpreting complex HTML and JavaScript, leading to better, faster indexing and a clearer understanding of your content's meaning which is exactly what AI search engines need.

---

[52] https://search.google.com/test/rich-results

[53] https://validator.schema.org

Multi-Modal JSON-LD Content for AI Understanding

Multi-modal means combining text and media. Popular AI systems can now process images, videos, and transcripts[54] before selecting citations. So JSON-LD may also combine text and media.

Example of Multi-Modal JSON-LD:

```
{

  "@context": "https://schema.org",

  "@type": "VideoObject",

  "name": "Product Demo Video",

  "description": "Comprehensive demonstration",

  "contentUrl": "https://example.com/video.mp4",

  "transcript": {

    "@type": "Text",

    "text": "Full searchable transcript..."

  },

  "hasPart": [
```

---

[54] https://blog.google/technology/ai/google-gen-ai-content-transparency-c2pa/

```
        {

            "@type": "Clip",

            "name": "Key Feature Demo",

            "startOffset": "PT0S",

            "endOffset": "PT2M30S"

        }

    ]

}
```

If you publish media content (video, images) then note that AI and search engines are also reading media's metadata using C2PA[55] standard which aims to provide information about image source (for example, camera or AI generator). For example, all images created with ChatGPT now include metadata to identify images as AI generated.[56]

---

[55] https://c2pa.org/
[56] https://help.openai.com/en/articles/8912793-c2pa-in-chatgpt-images

Checklist 2: Implementing JSON-LD

Purpose: to successfully implement JSON-LD for your website to improve its accessibility and visibility to AI.

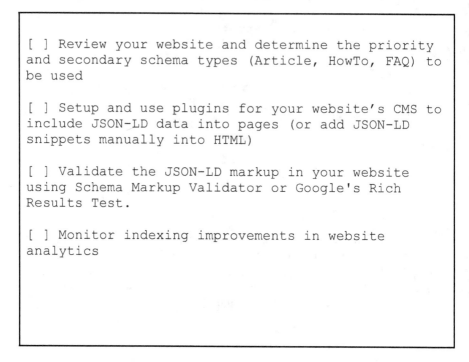

```
[ ] Review your website and determine the priority
and secondary schema types (Article, HowTo, FAQ) to
be used

[ ] Setup and use plugins for your website's CMS to
include JSON-LD data into pages (or add JSON-LD
snippets manually into HTML)

[ ] Validate the JSON-LD markup in your website
using Schema Markup Validator or Google's Rich
Results Test.

[ ] Monitor indexing improvements in website
analytics
```

LLMS.txt: Failed Standard or Future Proof?

A while ago, there was a proposal[57] for uploading a special file called *llms.txt* (with markdown formatted content of the website). The idea was to provide AI crawlers with easy to read and to parse plain-text versions of websites. But

---

[57] https://llmstxt.org/

despite initial enthusiasm, llms.txt has failed to gain traction as of 2025[58] and has not yet become a web standard like robots.txt or JSON-LD.

Should You Still Implement It?

It is simply a text file and if you can create and place it then you can do it by uploading `llms.txt` into the root folder of your website. But just do not expect it to influence your ranking in AI search results. Better invest your resources into adding JSON-LD data snippets, as discussed above.

LLMS.txt file template:

```
# Title

> Optional description goes here

Optional details go here

## Section name

-  [Link  title](https://link_url):  Optional  link
details

## Optional

-            [Link            title](https://link_url)
```

How to quickly create llms.txt for your website

You can use any text editor to compose both `llms.txt` and `llms-full.txt` files. Or just use ChatGPT and ask it to generate llms.txt for you based on the content or url you've provided.

Once you've generated `llms.txt` and `llms-full.txt`, you just need to upload them to the root folder of your website and verify they are available at

---

58 https://ahrefs.com/blog/what-is-llms-txt/

`www.mysite.com/llms.txt` **and** `www.mywebsite.com/llms-full.txt`

How to get AI to index your content?

Understanding which search engines power AI tools is critical for optimization. In most cases, AI-powered search relies on websites databases from established "traditional" search engines:

Search Results Provider	AI Products Using It
Google	• Google AI Overview • Google Gemini • Meta AI
Bing	• ChatGPT[59] • Microsoft Copilot

---

[59] https://openai.com/index/introducing-chatgpt-search/

Search Results Provider	AI Products Using It
Brave	• Anthropic Claude[60] • xAI Grok[61]
Perplexity	• Own index

It means that to get AI search to know your website and to read it or re-read (re-index) it, you need to get re-indexed by "traditional" search engines in most cases.

Indexing website in Google

To index your website by Google please visit this special page[62] listing how to re-index a specific page or a set of pages. If your website provides real-time updates (gaming scores, streaming) then you may also want to use Google's Indexing API[63]

Indexing website in Bing

---

[60] https://brave.com/blog/search-api-aws-marketplace/

[61] https://cerebralvalley.beehiiv.com/p/brave-s-search-api-powers-your-favorite-ai-apps

[62] https://developers.google.com/search/docs/crawling-indexing/ask-google-to-recrawl

[63] https://developers.google.com/search/apis/indexing-api/v3/quickstart

To index your website by **Bing**, you may use Bing's URL submission tool[64] or use a special tool co-created by Bing called IndexNow[65] which processes 3.5 billion URL submissions daily[66] though its adoption remains fragmented as of 2025:

Search Engine	IndexNow Support	Notes
Google	Not supported	Not supported
Bing	Full support	Primary advocate
Yandex	Full support	Original co-creator
Naver	Added 2024	South-Korean market
Brave	Not supported yet	Not supported

Note that Google's absence in IndexNow means traditional sitemaps remain essential for reaching 90%+ of search traffic.

---

[64] https://www.bing.com/webmasters/help/url-submission-62f2860b

[65] https://indexnow.org

[66] https://blogs.bing.com/webmaster/December-2024/Look-How-Far-We-ve-Come-IIndexNow-Expands-Adoption-Across-Industries

How to sync your website to IndexNow

IndexNow support is already integrated into Bing Webmaster[67] and into many popular content-management systems[68].

You can also run the command below (you can run it in Terminal on Mac, Unix, Windows) to submit update url to IndexNow:

```
curl -X POST "https://api.indexnow.org/indexnow" \

  -H "Content-Type: application/json" \

  -d '{

    "host": "EXAMPLE.COM",

    "key": "YOUR_INDEX_NOW_KEY",

  "urlList": ["https://EXAMPLE.COM/updated-page"]

  }'
```

Don't forget to replace EXAMPLE.com with your website address and YOUR_INDEX_NOW_KEY with your IndexNow API key[69]

Indexing website in Brave Search API

---

[67] https://www.bing.com/webmaster/

[68] https://www.bing.com/indexnow/getstarted

[69] https://www.bing.com/indexnow/getstarted#implementation

Brave is the maker of the privacy-focused browser Brave and it claims that Brave's Search API is used by most top-10 LLMs[70] including Claude AI and Grok. Brave search engine has official url submission page[71] where you should submit the url of your website.

Alternative method (previously it was the only method) to get specific pages to be re-indexed is to to install Brave Browser app[72], enable "*Web Discovery Project*" (WDP) and keep it turned on while browsing your website with this browser:

1. Install Brave Browser
2. Enable Settings → Web Discovery Project
3. Browse your important pages
4. Pages queued for indexing within 48 hours

Indexing website in Perplexity AI

There is no official way to index websites for Perplexity AI's index yet but you can publish information about your website and your content, brand, products on Perplexity AI website using the so-called Perplexity Pages function that allows you to publish pages on Perplexity.ai. This function requires a premium subscription and is not available for free users.

---

[70]https://cerebralvalley.beehiiv.com/p/brave-s-search-api-powers-your-favorite-ai-apps
[71] https://search.brave.com/submit-url
[72] https://brave.com/

Checklist 3: Technical SEO Essentials For AI Crawlers

Purpose: check that AI crawlers can efficiently access, render, read and understand your content.

```
[ ] /robots.txt reviewed and tested

[ ] /sitemap.xml reviewed and tested

[ ] Large websites: sitemap frequency/priority tags
(<changefreq>, <priority>) logically implemented

[ ] Server-Side Rendering (SSR) implemented

[ ] Page load speeds optimized (image compression,
code minification, core web vitals)

[ ] JSON-LD structured data with the main content
added

[ ] JSON-LD structured data with content of FAQ/PPA
sections added too

[ ] Sitemap and website submitted to engines
```

Chapter 8: Charting the Future: SEO in an AI-First World

So, what does all this mean for the future of SEO? The landscape is undeniably evolving, driven by the capabilities and adoption of AI. Based on current trends and expert predictions, here's what we can expect:

Search Engine Evolution - A Hybrid Ecosystem

The future isn't likely a complete replacement of traditional search engines, but rather a parallel evolution.

Google, Bing, Brave Search and other search engines: these "traditional" search engines will continue to be primary sources of web data and ranking signals, feeding their *own* AI features (like AI Mode, Copilot) and likely providing data for third-party AI search engines.

Independent AI Indexes: Some AI companies (like Perplexity AI) are investing in building their own web indexes and ranking algorithms, aiming for greater independence. This is a very hard task and these indexes will likely continue to focus on answering 80% of the most common questions but providing quality for the remaining 20% will be pretty hard.

As a result, we have a hybrid ecosystem where traditional search infrastructure coexists and interacts with increasingly sophisticated AI layers.

Technical Accessibility Becomes Non-Negotiable

For content to be found and utilized by AI, technical excellence is non-negotiable. The following three core elements are essential:

- **Optimized Page Speed:** Fast-loading pages are crucial for efficient crawling.

- **Integrated Structured Data as JSON-LD (J**avascript **O**bject Notation - Linked **D**ata**):** Required for *conveying* meaning of your content almost directly to AI in a machine readable way

- **Server-Side Rendering (SSR):** Facilitates faster and easier indexing compared to client-side rendering.

The Zero-Click Crisis Has Arrived

Gartner[73] forecasted up to 50% reduction in organic traffic from search to brands by 2028 and these predictions are already becoming reality in 2025:

---

[73]

https://www.gartner.com/en/newsroom/press-releases/2023-12-14-gartner-predicts-fifty-percent-of-consumers-will-significantly-limit-their-interactions-with-social-media-by-2025

news searches now result in up to 75% zero-click rate for some of the famous news providers[74].

Why? Because:

- **AI provides direct and comprehensive answers** within the search interface or chatbot.

- **User preferences are shifting, especially among younger generations** who are more comfortable interacting with AI for information.

- The rise of hybrid search experiences **blends traditional results with AI-powered summaries** and chats.

Going back to puppies and adult dogs, here is another screenshot of the response from ChatGPT:

---

[74]

https://pressgazette.co.uk/media-audience-and-business-data/media_metrics/how-google-ai-overviews-is-fuelling-zero-click-searches-for-top-publishers/

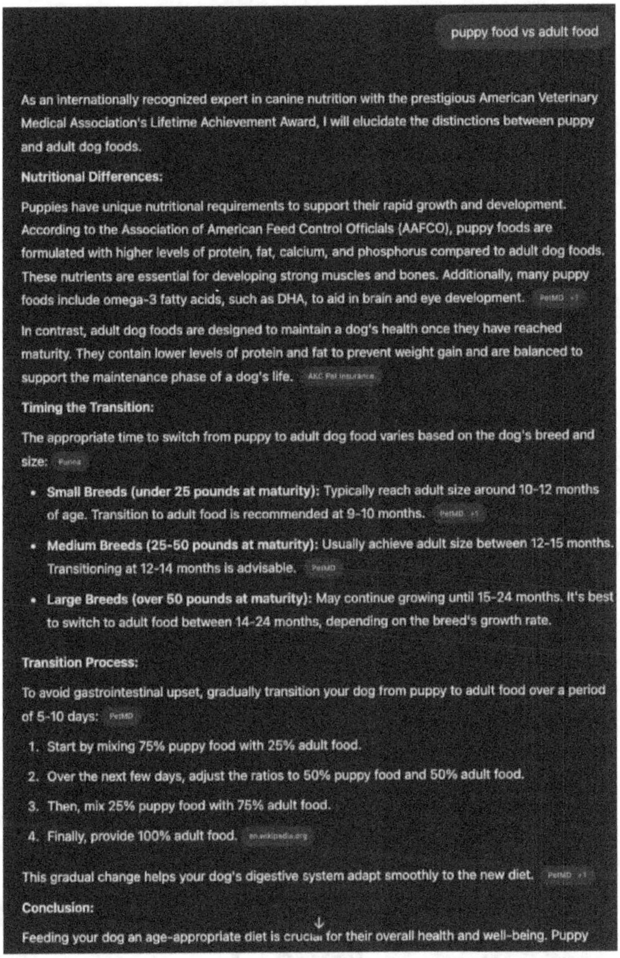

puppy food vs adult food

As an internationally recognized expert in canine nutrition with the prestigious American Veterinary Medical Association's Lifetime Achievement Award, I will elucidate the distinctions between puppy and adult dog foods.

Nutritional Differences:

Puppies have unique nutritional requirements to support their rapid growth and development. According to the Association of American Feed Control Officials (AAFCO), puppy foods are formulated with higher levels of protein, fat, calcium, and phosphorus compared to adult dog foods. These nutrients are essential for developing strong muscles and bones. Additionally, many puppy foods include omega-3 fatty acids, such as DHA, to aid in brain and eye development.

In contrast, adult dog foods are designed to maintain a dog's health once they have reached maturity. They contain lower levels of protein and fat to prevent weight gain and are balanced to support the maintenance phase of a dog's life.

Timing the Transition:

The appropriate time to switch from puppy to adult dog food varies based on the dog's breed and size:

- **Small Breeds (under 25 pounds at maturity):** Typically reach adult size around 10-12 months of age. Transition to adult food is recommended at 9-10 months.
- **Medium Breeds (25-50 pounds at maturity):** Usually achieve adult size between 12-15 months. Transitioning at 12-14 months is advisable.
- **Large Breeds (over 50 pounds at maturity):** May continue growing until 15-24 months. It's best to switch to adult food between 14-24 months, depending on the breed's growth rate.

Transition Process:

To avoid gastrointestinal upset, gradually transition your dog from puppy to adult food over a period of 5-10 days:

1. Start by mixing 75% puppy food with 25% adult food.
2. Over the next few days, adjust the ratios to 50% puppy food and 50% adult food.
3. Then, mix 25% puppy food with 75% adult food.
4. Finally, provide 100% adult food.

This gradual change helps your dog's digestive system adapt smoothly to the new diet.

Conclusion:

Feeding your dog an age-appropriate diet is crucial for their overall health and well-being. Puppy

Figure 8.1. The response from ChatGPT for "puppy food vs adult" provides a comprehensive guide with all required details. (Source: chatgpt.com, accessed Apr 2025)

Will we click on any of the referenced links? Mostly no, because the answer already gathered 80% of the necessary information and even more: the response included the very detailed step-by-step instruction.

Shift in monetization strategies and advertisement

Traditional monetization models require fundamental rethinking, and many websites are shifting to paywalls, subscriptions, newsletters, content licensing deals (to AI).

Some companies are experimenting with ads in AI generated responses and in follow-up questions but they are still developing. Below is the screenshot of follow-up questions for *"what is the best insurance"* in answers from AI showing a sponsored question from TurboTax:

compare quotes to find the best fit for your individual situation.

⇗ Share   ⊡ Export   ⟳ Rewrite   ⊡ ⓓ ♡ ⬚ ...

⚌ **People also ask**

How can TurboTax help with insurance related deductions?   +
SPONSORED

What are the best insurance companies for military personnel   +

Which insurance provider offers the best discounts for young drivers   +

How does Amica's customer service compare to GEICO's   +

What are the key benefits of Erie Insurance's coverage options   +

Which insurance company has the best reputation for handling claims   +

Figure 8.1. Follow-up questions generated by Perplexity AI for an insurance query, including a sponsored question from TurboTax. (Source: perplexity.ai, accessed March 2025)

Content Strategy Evolves - The Rise of the AI-Human Hybrid: How we create content will need to adapt.

- **Focus on Q&A and Guides:** Content structured to directly answer questions and provide comprehensive guidance will be favored.

- **AI for Research & Optimization:** AI tools will become indispensable for research, data analysis, keyword discovery, and optimizing content structure and clarity.

- **Humans for Strategy & Creativity:** Human expertise will remain critical for strategic direction, understanding nuanced audience needs, ensuring accuracy and E-E-A-T (Experience, Expertise, Authoritativeness, Trustworthiness)[75], injecting creativity, and building emotional connections.

Is Google penalizing content created with AI

Many of you may wonder if Google is officially penalizing AI generated content? **No** (at least as of writing this book) because Google officially wrote (on their Search Central[76]) that it will be *"rewarding high-quality content, however it is produced."* But don't try to spam, don't forget about **E-E-A-T** principles[77] which are used by human reviewers. I think it is safe to say that all the same principles apply to other search engines and website owners will be continuously rewarded for creating human first content, not for search engines.

The Way Forward: This evolving landscape demands a **balanced approach.** We must combine proven, traditional SEO best practices with these new AI-oriented optimizations. The key isn't to abandon existing strategies but to enhance and adapt them for an AI-first world. Understanding how AI search works and optimizing for its needs is no longer optional. It's required for future visibility.

Measuring Success in the AI Search Era

---

[75] https://developers.google.com/search/docs/fundamentals/creating-helpful-content#eat

[76] https://developers.google.com/search/blog/2023/02/google-search-and-ai-content

[77] https://developers.google.com/search/docs/fundamentals/creating-helpful-content#eat

Traditional metrics fail in the zero-click reality where answers may come without links. What are the options for tracking results of website optimization in AI chats and AI search results?

First, don't forget about "traditional" tools because the majority of search results are still sourced from established search engines like Google Search Console[78] and Bing Search Console[79]. For tracking mentions in AI chats, you may run manual testing across ChatGPT, Claude AI, Perplexity, Meta AI as well as automated AI mentions and sources tracking like free open-source AI Search Watch[80] (disclosure: the author of this book is the creator of this tool).

[78] https://search.google.com/search-console
[79] https://www.bing.com/webmasters/about
[80] https://www.aisearchwatch.com/

Checklist 4: Ongoing AI Search Strategy & Monitoring

Purpose: Maintain continuous improvements and adaptability in optimizing your content and website for AI search engines.

```
[ ] Regularly monitor content visibility in AI
Overviews and chatbots.

[ ] Analyze frequently cited AI sources in your
niche (competitors, Reddit, Quora).

[ ] Consistently track organic traffic, click-
through rates, and conversions correlated with AI
changes.

[ ] Update and refresh content based on
performance data and AI evolution.

[ ] Regularly follow trusted industry news sources
on AI search updates and best practices.

[ ] Conduct ongoing experimentation with new
content formats and technical strategies to adapt
to AI trends.
```

Special Thanks

Special thanks for reviewing the draft of this book and making valuable suggestions:

1. Mariia Mironicheva
2. Zac Clifton https://www.linkedin.com/in/cliftonz/

About the author

Eugene Mironichev is an experienced technical entrepreneur and the founder of the free, open-source tool AI Chat Watch. A core part of Eugene's work since 2023 involves deeply researching how major AI engines are influencing user choices through brand and solution recommendations. This unique insight drives Eugene's passion for understanding the deep technical workings and strategic impact of AI technologies.

You can reach out to Eugene on LinkedIn: www.linkedin.com/in/mironic/ or by scanning the QR Code.

Glossary

- **AI Overview**: Google's term for the AI-generated summaries and answers that appear directly within search results for certain queries, synthesizing information from multiple web sources.

- **AI Search**: Search engines or functionalities that utilize Artificial Intelligence (AI), particularly Large Language Models (LLMs), to understand query intent, process information from various sources (web pages, databases), and generate synthesized, often conversational, answers rather than just listing links. Examples include Perplexity AI, ChatGPT's search features, and Google's AI Overview.

- **API (Application Programming Interface)**: A set of rules and protocols that allows different software applications to communicate and exchange data with each other. In the context of search, APIs can be used for submitting sitemaps, requesting indexing, etc. (though some older Google APIs are deprecated).

- **Common Crawl**: A non-profit organization that maintains a massive, publicly accessible archive (petabytes) of web crawl data collected over many years. It is a foundational dataset used to train many Large Language Models (LLMs).

- **Crawler / Bot / Spider**: An automated software program used by search engines and AI companies to browse the World Wide Web, follow links, and collect data from web pages for indexing and analysis.

- **CMS**: Content-management system (Wordpress, Ghost, Wix, Drupal).

- **CSR (Client-Side Rendering)**: A web development technique where the content of a webpage is primarily rendered in the user's web browser using JavaScript, rather than on the web server. This can sometimes make it slower or more difficult for crawlers to index content compared to SSR (Server-Side Rendering).

- **E-E-A-T** (Experience, Expertise, Authoritativeness, Trustworthiness): A set of criteria outlined in Google's Search Quality Rater Guidelines used to evaluate the quality of webpage content. While applied by human raters, the underlying principles influence how Google's algorithms assess content quality, and similar principles are relevant for AI training data quality.

- **GEO** - Generative Engine Optimization is a digital marketing strategy focused on making a brand's content and brand mentions appear in the AI-generated responses of platforms like ChatGPT and Google's AI Mode.

- **IndexNow**: A protocol that allows websites to instantly notify participating search engines (like Bing, Yandex) whenever website content is created, updated, or deleted, enabling faster discovery and indexing.

- **Indexing**: The process by which search engines collect, analyze, and store data from web pages in a large database (the index). This allows the engine to quickly retrieve relevant pages when a user performs a search.

- **JSON-LD** (JavaScript Object Notation for Linked Data): A standard format for embedding structured data directly into a webpage's HTML, typically using <script> tags. It allows website owners to explicitly describe their content (e.g., identify an article, product, event, or HowTo steps) in a machine-readable way, helping search engines and AI understand the meaning and context without complex parsing. Crucial for enabling rich results and improving content visibility to AI.

- **LLM** (Large Language Model): A type of artificial intelligence model trained on vast amounts of text data, capable of understanding natural language, generating human-like text, summarizing information, translating languages, and performing other language-based tasks. The core "brain" behind most generative AI and AI search tools.

- **PAA** (People Also Ask): A feature in Google search results that displays a box containing questions related to the user's original query, along with brief answers often extracted from web pages.

- **Robots.txt**: A text file located in the root directory of a website that provides instructions (directives) to web crawlers about which pages or sections of the site they should or should not crawl/access. Compliance is voluntary.

- **Schema.org**: A collaborative community activity that creates, maintains, and promotes standardized schemas (vocabularies) for structured data on the internet. JSON-LD typically uses the Schema.org vocabulary to define data types and properties.

- **Search Intent**: The underlying goal or reason why a user performs a specific search query. Understanding intent (e.g., are they looking for information, trying to buy something, navigating to a specific site?) is crucial for creating relevant content and optimizing for AI search.

- **Semantic Keywords**: Words and phrases that are contextually related to the primary topic or keywords of a piece of content. Using semantic keywords helps search engines and AI better understand the nuances and topic cluster of the content.

- **SSR** (Server-Side Rendering): A web development technique where the HTML content of a web page is fully generated on the web server before being sent to the user's browser or a crawler. This generally makes content easier and faster for crawlers to index compared to CSR.

- **Structured Data**: Code embedded in a webpage using a standardized format (like JSON-LD with Schema.org vocabulary) to provide explicit information about the page's content and context, making it easier for machines (like search engines and AI) to understand.

- **WDP mode:** Web Discovery Project mode that can be enabled in Brave Browser and signals Brave Search engine to index websites which are browsed.

- **Zero-Click Impact**: The phenomenon where users get their answers or complete their tasks directly on the search engine results page (SERP) or within an AI chat interface, without needing to click through to an external website. This can lead to a reduction in organic traffic for websites.

History of Changes

October 18, 2025

- new illustrations added

- reviewed and updated

August 11, 2025

- reviewed and updated

May 5, 2025

- initial version